Captivating Lateral
Thinking Puzzles

Official **MENSA**®
Puzzle Book

Captivating Lateral Thinking Puzzles

PAUL SLOANE & DES MacHALE

ILLUSTRATED BY STEVE MACK

STERLING

New York / London
www.sterlingpublishing.com

Edited by Francis Heaney
Illustrated by Steve Mack

Library of Congress Cataloging-in-Publication Data Available

STERLING and the distinctive Sterling logo are registered trademarks of
Sterling Publishing Co., Inc.

Mensa and the distinctive table logo are registered trademarks of
American Mensa, Ltd. (in the U.S.),
British Mensa, Ltd. (in the U.K.),
Australian Mensa, Inc. (in Australia),
and Mensa International Limited (in other countries)
and are used by permission.

2   4   6   8   10   9   7   5   3   1

Published by Sterling Publishing Co., Inc.
387 Park Avenue South, New York, NY 10016
© 2007 by Paul Sloane and Des MacHale
Distributed in Canada by Sterling Publishing
c/o Canadian Manda Group, 165 Dufferin Street
Toronto, Ontario, Canada M6K 3H6
Distributed in the United Kingdom by GMC Distribution Services
Castle Place, 166 High Street, Lewes, East Sussex, England BN7 1XU
Distributed in Australia by Capricorn Link (Australia) Pty. Ltd.
P.O. Box 704, Windsor, NSW 2756, Australia

Sterling ISBN-13: 978-1-4027-3276-8
ISBN-10: 1-4027-3276-7

For information about custom editions, special sales, premium and
corporate purchases, please contact Sterling Special Sales
Department at 800-805-5489 or specialsales@sterlingpublishing.com.

Dedicated to Toby Phelps

ACKNOWLEDGMENTS

Thanks to
Dean Ryman for "Well Done,"
Barbara Bailey for "Lying Dead,"
Lloyd King for "Twin Peeks"
and "Getting Away With Murder,"
and Michael O'Fiachra for "Watch Out."
Thanks also to all contributors to the Lateral
Puzzles Forum at www.lateralpuzzles.com.

CONTENTS

INTRODUCTION

In the wonderful old movie *The 39 Steps*, the hero, Richard Hannay, is trapped in a packed theater. He is surrounded by enemy agents and police, who are blocking every entrance and exit to the theater, even the wings of the stage. Logically, it would appear that he has no means of escape—he is outnumbered and there is no path to freedom. But that conclusion comes from dull linear thinking, sequential logic that slavishly points in just one direction.

Enter lateral thinking, an exciting and highly nonlinear form of thought that looks at situations from a totally different point of view and often finds a hidden dynamic in a problem by means of which it can be solved. Interestingly, this solution can depend on the clever use of the obstruction that is causing the problem in the first place!

So what did Richard Hannay do to escape? Well, thinking laterally, he lit a match and shouted "Fire, fire!" In panic, the huge audience surged towards the exits, sweeping the police and enemy agents away. In the resulting chaos, our hero escaped. As in many instances, the solution is devastatingly simple once you see it.

In this book we invite you once again to partake in the joys of lateral thinking by considering dozens of brand new lateral thinking puzzles we have made up just for your pleasure. You will be presented with many scenarios which are unusual, extraordinary, or even bizarre, and your task is to find out what is going on, why the described events are taking place, or how come these seemingly contradictory events have unfolded. If you can solve them without any help, then you are indeed a lateral thinking genius, but we have provided clues just in case you get stuck.

If you want to play the Lateral Thinking Game, then a chairperson who has read the solution can give participants answers to questions consisting of the words "yes," "no," or "irrelevant."

If this is all new to you, you are in for a rare treat, but even if you are a seasoned lateral puzzle cracker, we guarantee you we have quite a few new tricks up our sleeves. So have a great lateral time with these new puzzles, and remember—we love making them up just as much as you love solving them!

PUZZLES

Well Done

The teacher said "Bravo, Juliet," to his pupil but in fact he was very displeased. Why?

Find clues on p. 50 and the answer on p. 72.

Twin Peeks

Jasmine's two best friends, Josh and Phoenix, are twins and always look identical—they even wear matching clothes. While walking to school Jasmine noticed one of the twins walking ahead of her. Not knowing whether it was Josh or Phoenix, she called out, "Hi there." As soon as he turned to face her she knew it was Phoenix. How did she know?

Find clues on p. 50 and the answer on p. 72.

Bee Trail

A woman died because of a bee. It did not sting her. How did she die?

Find clues on p. 50 and the answer on p. 72.

Can the Can

A man always carried a canister of deadly poison with him. Why?

Find clues on p. 50 and the answer on p. 72.

The Bathtub Test

There is a bathtub filled with water. On the bathroom counter are the following items: a teaspoon, a cup, a length of rubber hose, and a bucket. You have to empty the bathtub as quickly as possible. Which of the methods available to you should you use?

Find clues on p. 50 and the answer on p. 72.

Defective Dismissal

A man reported to his boss that a certain piece of equipment he was operating was mildly defective. The boss immediately fired him. Why?

Find clues on p. 51 and the answer on p. 72.

Dampened Spirits

Why did a man deliberately wet his pants?

Find clues on p. 51 and the answer on p. 73.

Buttons

What was the original reason that little buttons were sewn on the sleeves of men's jackets?

Find clues on p. 51 and the answer on p. 73.

Stage Fright

Why did a really bad play attract thousands of theatergoers week after week?

Find clues on p. 51 and the answer on p. 73.

The Warm Prisoner

A man is imprisoned in a prison cell with no window. The cell is warm and heated. He has no radio, TV, or phone, and the cell is in solitary confinement, so he speaks with nobody (not even the guards, who are forbidden to communicate with him). Yet he can tell that it's very cold outside. How does he know?

Find clues on p. 51 and the answer on p. 73.

Tight Fit

A woman bought a pair of shoes that were too small for her. She wore them anyway. Why?

Find clues on p. 52 and the answer on p. 73.

On the Loose

Why is it that the male pilots in the air force generally wear bigger shirts than the male mechanics, even when they are off duty?

Find clues on p. 52 and the answer on p. 73.

Fingered

A burglar, who is wearing a pair of gloves, enters a house he has never been in before. He does not remove the gloves until he returns home after successfully making off with lots of valuable jewelry. However, he is caught because he left his fingerprints on the safe he robbed. How did that happen?

Find clues on p. 52 and the answer on p. 74.

Lots of Dough

A baker in Connecticut in the 19th century was in the habit of giving his employees an hour off for lunch in which to amuse themselves. This resulted in the creation of a multi-million dollar business. What is it?

Find clues on p. 52 and the answer on p. 74.

A Sight for Sore Eyes

How did the advice about eating carrots to improve your eyesight originate?

Find clues on p. 52 and the answer on p. 74.

Getting Away With Murder

A security guard in a hotel sees a man go into a room in which there is no one else present and which may only be accessed through a single doorway. Several minutes later he sees a woman enter the room and immediately scream. Lying dead in a pool of blood in the room is the man, murdered. But how did the killer get into and out of the room without being seen by the guard, who had remained on the same spot and watchful throughout?

Find clues on p. 53 and the answer on p. 75.

Sparkle

A former U.S. president was sometimes known to brush his teeth five separate times in a single morning. Why?

Find clues on p. 53 and the answer on p. 75.

Awfully Unlawful

Why is it illegal for a man to knit a sweater on the island of Jersey?

Find clues on p. 53 and the answer on p. 75.

Bow Untied

The actor Pierce Brosnan played the lead role in a movie called *The Thomas Crown Affair*. In it he appears in a scene at a nightclub and he wears a white bow tie which is undone. He could not have worn a black bow tie (tied or untied) if he wanted to. Why not?

Find clues on p. 53 and the answer on p. 75.

Ageism

• •

The senior center was having a problem with uninvited high schoolers who loitered on the porch and would sit in the kitchen and help themselves to snacks. What did the authorities do that deterred the youngsters without bothering the senior citizens?

Find clues on p. 54 and the answer on p. 75.

Bad News

• •

Jane heard a news item about a famous actress and immediately knew it was incorrect, but she could not do anything about it. Why not?

Find clues on p. 54 and the answer on p. 76.

Nipped in Nippy Weather

A drug dealer was very careful to hide his activities. However, in cold weather his crimes were discovered. How?

Find clues on p. 54 and the answer on p. 76.

Victoriana 1

What item in the Victorian wardrobe was six times as big as its modern equivalent?

Find clues on p. 54 and the answer on p. 76.

Victoriana 2

What live animal was found in many Victorian kitchens but is never seen in kitchens today?

Find clues on p. 54 and the answer on p. 76.

Shammin' Famine

During the 1950s the Chinese did not allow foreign journalists to visit the countryside, so that the world would not know about serious famines there. Journalists were only allowed to go to a handful of large cities that appeared relatively prosperous. How did one Russian journalist deduce there was actually a famine in the countryside?

Find clues on p. 55 and the answer on p. 77.

Come Home Quick

After a heavily attended rugby match, the mayor of Limerick begged all the fans from his city to return home as soon as possible. Why?

Find clues on p. 55 and the answer on p. 77.

I Spy

A German spy lands in America during World War II. He speaks excellent English. How is he found out by the authorities?

Find clues on p. 55 and the answer on p. 77.

Lying Dead

A man is lying dead on a beach. What happened?

Find clues on p. 55 and the answer on p. 77.

Passed With Extinction

In 1925 there were 200,000,000 of them. In 2005 there were 21,000 of them. In 2006 there were none. What are they?

Find clues on p. 55 and the answer on p. 77.

Back Again

A man working in an office is fired from his job. Why does he show up at the office early the next morning?

Find clues on p. 56 and the answer on p. 78.

Definitely Not

A newspaperman reporting in Albania wanted to find a native Albanian to interview, but every time he asked someone if they had been born in Albania, they firmly shook their head from side to side, and he moved on. Why was the reporter having such a hard time?

Find clues on p. 56 and the answer on p. 78.

Nervous Wreck

A ship sank in 20-foot-deep water, blocking the entrance to a harbor. All efforts to raise it failed until a sports shop owner came up with an idea that did the trick. What did he suggest?

Find clues on p. 56 and the answer on p. 78.

Singles

....

Why did one member of a band insist on being paid in single dollar bills only?

Find clues on p. 56 and the answer on p. 78.

Amadeus

....

Mozart wrote five movements for the suite *Eine Kleine Nachtmusik* but only four of them are ever played on the radio. Why?

Find clues on p. 57 and the answer on p. 78.

Let's Split

Why did 9 out of every 10 couples in a small Chinese village suddenly get divorced?

Find clues on p. 57 and the answer on p. 78.

Elongation

For one week, Ben was three inches taller than he was before or after. How come?

Find clues on p. 57 and the answer on p. 79.

Ring-a-Ding

A woman heard a bell ring and knew that she had lost a lot of money, but she was still delighted. Why?

Find clues on p. 57 and the answer on p. 79.

Wet Coffee

When you are served a coffee in Cyprus, it is traditional to add a little water to it. Why?

Find clues on p. 58 and the answer on p. 79.

Truffle Snuffle

Why are dogs now being used instead of pigs to sniff out the truffles, the precious fungi loved by gourmets?

Find clues on p. 58 and the answer on p. 80.

Sell-by Date

What food found in the Great Pyramids was still edible?

Find clues on p. 58 and the answer on p. 80.

Fly by Night

Traditionally it is not allowed for the U.S. flag to be hung at full mast outdoors at night, except in one place. Where?

Find clues on p. 58 and the answer on p. 80.

The Odd Day

How does Monday differ from every other day of the week?

Find clues on p. 58 and the answer on p. 80.

Break the Fall

A climber was climbing Mount Everest when he fell and broke his leg. How did he manage to complete the ascent?

Find clues on p. 59 and the answer on p. 80.

Faint-hearted

A man is lying in a hospital ward. A nurse comes in and tells him he is going home today. The man faints. Why?

Find clues on p. 59 and the answer on p. 81.

Pack Man

A man is found dead in a forest with a pack on his back. What had happened?

Find clues on p. 59 and the answer on p. 81.

A Strange Count

A man born in 1947 died in 1984 at the age of 55. How come?

Find clues on p. 59 and the answer on p. 81.

Ready, Teddy

Why were a man and a woman walking around, each carrying a large teddy bear?

Find clues on p. 59 and the answer on p. 81.

Strike a Light

French troops fighting in the trenches at night were afraid to light matches by which to read messages and orders from headquarters because enemies might spot them. What did Charles Babier suggest that solved the problem but had vastly more important consequences for millions of people?

Find clues on p. 60 and the answer on p. 81.

Pay Dirt

∙∙∙

Two men escaped from prison by digging an 80-foot tunnel from their cell to the outside. What did they do with the dirt from the tunnel?

Find clues on p. 60 and the answer on p. 81.

Two Women

∙∙∙

The same thing happened to two women, one living in New York and the other living in London. The woman in New York was delighted, but the woman in London was very upset. Why?

Find clues on p. 60 and the answer on p. 82.

Toy Wreck

A ship crossing the Atlantic Ocean with a huge cargo of children's toys sank in a storm. Why was this tragedy of great use to scientists?

Find clues on p. 60 and the answer on p. 82.

Just Four Words

A king was annoyed with his jester and threatened to execute him. He gave the jester the following task as a chance to save his skin: "Design a bracelet to put on my wrist with just four four-letter words on it. When I am sad the inscription must make me happy, and when I am happy the inscription must make me sad." What did the jester have inscribed on the bracelet?

Find clues on p. 61 and the answer on p. 82.

Murderous Intent

A woman meets the man of her dreams at her mother's funeral but she neglects to get his name, address, or any other contact details. A few days later she kills her sister. Why?

Find clues on p. 61 and the answer on p. 82.

Ford Car

Why was a car floating down a river with two very annoyed passengers on board?

Find clues on p. 61 and the answer on p. 82.

Fair Enough

••

When the exiled king of Norway made a wartime broadcast to his subjects on BBC Radio, the transmission was accompanied by a short segment of fairground noises. Why?

Find clues on p. 61 and the answer on p. 82.

Hide and Seek

••

A spy is tipped off that the police will raid and search his house the next morning to find and confiscate his secret codebook. There is nobody he trusts enough to give it to, so where does he hide it for safekeeping?

Find clues on p. 61 and the answer on p. 82.

Monkey Business

To what useful medical use are marmoset monkeys put in some parts of Africa?

Find clues on p. 62 and the answer on p. 83.

Unconventional

Why were members of a religious order strictly forbidden to say "hello" to each other?

Find clues on p. 62 and the answer on p. 83.

That Sinking Feeling

When the Burgoyne sank in the Atlantic, all of the passengers were rescued except one. Why was he lost?

Find clues on p. 62 and the answer on p. 83.

Present Perfect

A mail order firm included a small gift with each order. Then they started including a different, less expensive gift, and found that this caused them to have more repeat customers. Why?

Find clues on p. 62 and the answer on p. 83.

Hose Down

Why and how did the fire service nearly destroy a collection of rare plants?

Find clues on p. 62 and the answer on p. 83.

Something You Don't See Every Day

In a town in the U.S. there is a statue honoring Hanson Gregory for inventing nothing. Why would this merit a statue?

Find clues on p. 63 and the answer on p. 83.

More Murderous Intent

A man wanted to commit suicide by shooting himself. His life insurance policy paid out if he died by accident or was murdered but not if he committed suicide. How did he make his death look like murder rather than suicide?

Find clues on p. 63 and the answer on p. 84.

Red, White, and Blue

France played Portugal in the semifinal of the soccer World Cup in 2006. The Portuguese team wore red. French teams normally wear blue but this time they were not allowed to wear blue and played in white instead. Why?

Find clues on p. 63 and the answer on p. 84.

Upgrade Upset

John and Jane were thrilled to be upgraded to first class on their flight. But their pleasure quickly turned to embarrassment. Why?

Find clues on p. 63 and the answer on p. 84.

Untouchable

In an art gallery in London, there were several signs on an open display exhibit that read PLEASE DO NOT TOUCH ANY PART OF THIS EXHIBIT yet several people did touch a part of the exhibit. Why?

Find clues on p. 64 and the answer on p. 85.

Salt Fault

Why did a distinguished guest at a party take one of his hostess's prized salt shakers and put it into his pocket?

Find clues on p. 64 and the answer on p. 85.

Burnt Out

A man tells a woman that her kitchen is on fire and she gets angry. Why?

Find clues on p. 64 and the answer on p. 85.

The Angry Vacationer

A man returned from his vacation. He walked down his road to speak to a neighbor. Then he ran shouting angrily down the street. Why?

Find clues on p. 64 and the answer on p. 85.

No Business Like Sideshow Business

In the early days of Barnum's circus it is said that Barnum had a number of dubious attractions. One was described as a "Man Eating Fish" and another was a "Cherry-Colored Cat." What did people see when they paid to enter these tents?

Find clues on p. 64 and the answer on p. 85.

The Odd Shot

At a major golf tournament, a player's ball is in the rough. He has a clear view of the pin on the green, but he does not play his shot towards the green. He opts to chip out on to the fairway instead. Why?

Find clues on p. 65 and the answer on p. 86.

Cheers

A London man was diagnosed with cancer. As a result he was denied a drink in all the local bars. Why?

Find clues on p. 65 and the answer on p. 86.

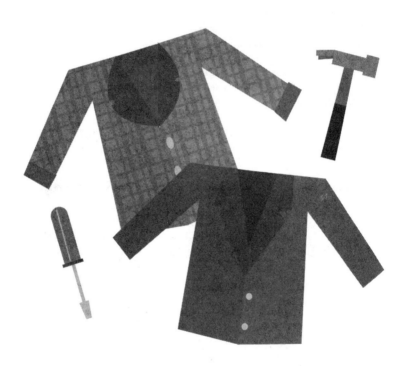

Two Coats

Why did Kevin wear two coats when he was repairing his house on a warm day?

Find clues on p. 65 and the answer on p. 86.

Go With the Flow

How can a river flow north one week and south the next week?

Find clues on p. 65 and the answer on p. 86.

No Charge

A woman goes into a store in the Mall of America, picks up an item, and attempts to pay for it with what is very obviously a homemade $200 bill. The storekeeper calls the police. The police, however, do not charge the woman with attempting to pass a counterfeit bill. Why?

Find clues on p. 65 and the answer on p. 86.

Rival Arrival

••

Antonia was hosting a high society ball. She heard that her social rival, Gwendoline, was planning to wear the same ball gown as Antonia. What did she do to upstage her foe?

Find clues on p. 66 and the answer on p. 86.

Skid Lids

••

Bicycle helmets are designed to increase safety and protection for cyclists. A recent report indicated that they might be achieving the opposite result. Why?

Find clues on p. 66 and the answer on p. 87.

Mouseophobia

Betty was absolutely terrified of mice, alive or dead. One day her cat came into the house with a mouse in his mouth and laid it at her feet. Instead of screaming, she calmly picked it up and threw it in the trash. Why?

Find clues on p. 66 and the answer on p. 87.

The Dunce

As a young boy, Sammy was always at the bottom of the class in mathematics, but in later life this fact worked to his advantage. How come?

Find clues on p. 66 and the answer on p. 87.

An Unwanted Purchase

A woman went into a shop and bought something that she did not need or want. The item was clearly defective, yet she paid full price for it. Why did she buy it?

Find clues on p. 66 and the answer on p. 88.

Watch Out

A man and a woman went into a restaurant for a meal. The waiter insisted that the man remove his wristwatch. Why?

Find clues on p. 67 and the answer on p. 88.

The Unfriendly Man

A man approached a woman he had never spoken to before and knew nothing about—he didn't know even her name. Suddenly he punched her violently in the face. Why?

Find clues on p. 67 and the answer on p. 88.

Parking Lark

Hugo heard a lie so he parked his pickup truck a long way away and walked home. Why?

Find clues on p. 67 and the answer on p. 89.

Stuck Fast

An explorer, traveling alone through treacherous country, got stuck in a narrow rock opening and could move neither up nor down. Unable to reach his cell phone and too far away from civilization to shout for help, how did he escape?

Find clues on p. 67 and the answer on p. 89.

What's the Hitch?

Rear Window is a movie directed by Alfred Hitchcock and starring James Stewart and Grace Kelly. What major mistake did Hitchcock make with the cast?

Find clues on p. 68 and the answer on p. 89.

Unorganized

A conference on world food supply was a huge success but it was described by a leading newspaper as "unorganized." Why?

Find clues on p. 68 and the answer on p. 90.

The Inventive Survivor

A man was in hotel room when a terrible fire broke out. He was trapped in his room on the 20th floor and the window did not open. Poisonous smoke was coming under the door and through the air conditioning system. He started to choke. If he could last another 10 minutes help would arrive. What did he do?

Find clues on p. 68 and the answer on p. 90.

Fishing Rods

Why did a woman push several fish into her curtain rods?

Find clues on p. 68 and the answer on p. 90.

Staying Grounded

Why did Patrick buy an airplane ticket to a foreign destination when he never had any intention of taking the trip?

Find clues on p. 69 and the answer on p. 91.

A Fishy Story

A man is an avid angler and spends a lot of his time fishing. A gossip tells his wife that her husband is only pretending to be away fishing, and is in fact having an affair. How does his wife know her husband is always where he says he is, fishing?

Find clues on p. 69 and the answer on p. 91.

Curses!

A frustrated schoolboy said a four-letter word in class. His teacher scolded him, but not for swearing. What for?

Find clues on p. 69 and the answer on p. 91.

WALLY Test

And now we present a test provided by the World Association of Learning, Laughter, and Youth (WALLY). Unlike the other puzzles in this book, which require thought and reflection, these are meant to be answered as quickly as possible. Give yourself two minutes to answer all ten, don't change any answers once you've written them down, then check the answer section to see how you did.

1. What's orange and sounds like a parrot?

2. In your head, take 1,000 and add 40 to it. Add another 1,000. Now add 30. Add another 1,000. Now add 20. Add another 1,000. Finally, add 10. What is the total?

3. What do you get if you halve 8?

4. Which movie star wore the same coat in every film?

5. Many of the planets in the solar system share the same characteristics—how many of the planets have earthquakes?

6. In what sport do half the contestants wear metal shoes?

7. What do you call people born in San Francisco?

8. Why could Al Capone never get out of prison?

9. Where does yesterday always come after today?

10. What should you do if you go into town and see a spaceman?

Find the answers on p. 92.

CLUES

Well Done

- The teacher was displeased with his pupil's work because she had made an error.

- His pupil's name was not Juliet.

- He gave her the right answer.

Twin Peeks

- Jasmine deduced correctly that it was Phoenix in front of her. But there was nothing in his appearance to distinguish him from his twin brother.

- She knew because he turned around.

Bee Trail

- The woman was not allergic to bees.

- The bee was a queen bee.

- The woman was a performer.

Can the Can

- He intended to use it but not for some evil purpose.

- It was not a weed or insect or pest killer.

- He used it outside the house but not on his garden or with animals.

- He used it with his car.

The Bathtub Test

- The bath is a normal bath—like yours!

- Choose the quickest method to empty the bath.

Defective Dismissal

- The man was dismissed for laziness.
- The equipment he was using was a wheelbarrow.
- He described its operation to the boss.

Dampened Spirits

- It was an emergency, but fire was not involved.
- His action helped him to escape.
- It was cold, but he did not need to thaw anything.

Buttons

- It was not for decoration.
- It was for a practical purpose, but nothing was ever fastened to the buttons.
- It was to prevent a bad habit.

Stage Fright

- The answer has nothing to do with the nature of the play, where it was performed, or who was in it.
- The critics all gave the play bad reviews.
- The ads for the play quoted glowing reviews, and the quotes were not taken out of context.

The Warm Prisoner

- He never leaves the cell.
- The clue that tells him it is cold outside is not a visible sign.
- It does not involve the floor, walls, or ceiling of the cell.
- Something in the cell does connect to the outside world.

Tight Fit
- The shoes caused her pain.
- The shoes helped her to do something.
- She wanted the shoes to cause her pain.

On the Loose
- The pilots and the mechanics are all completely normal men.
- This has nothing to do with anything that the pilots wear under or over their shirts.
- It does concern the equipment that the pilots use.

Fingered
- The burglar was not very bright.
- He left his fingerprints when he burgled the safe.
- He never took his gloves off.

Lots of Dough
- The employees' recreational activities resulted in a new sport or recreation, which is now enjoyed by millions.
- They used baking equipment.

A Sight for Sore Eyes
- It was a deliberate piece of deception.
- The story was not aimed at children nor was it originally designed to improve health or nutrition.
- It helped the war effort.

Getting Away With Murder
- The man did not kill himself. He was stabbed to death.
- The murderer was neither the woman nor the guard.
- The murderer entered and left the room.
- There was just one door and there were no windows or other entrances to the room.
- The room was very small.

Sparkle
- The man in question is Lyndon B. Johnson, although this was before he became president.
- He did not do it to improve oral hygiene or appearance nor did he do it for medical reasons.
- It helped his early career.

Awfully Unlawful
- Women are allowed to knit on Jersey.
- The reason has nothing to do with crime or health or risk of injury.
- This restriction was introduced to protect an essential industry.

Bow Untied
- Pierce Brosnan could not wear a black tie (or a tied bow tie of any color) but anyone else in that scene or that movie could do so.
- There would have been severe consequences to Brosnan if he had worn a black tie, but not of a physical nature.

Ageism

- They installed something that annoyed young people but went unnoticed by the senior citizens.

- The faculties of older people decline over time.

Bad News

- Jane was not related to the actress and had never met or contacted her.

- The actress was being dishonest and had provided the newspaper with incorrect information.

- The news concerned a crime.

Nipped in Nippy Weather

- He was not detected through information from his customers or from being observed selling drugs on the street.

- A neighbor noticed something about his house.

Victoriana 1

- It is something that is worn by both men and women.

- It is worn outdoors.

- The Victorians were more modest than we are.

Victoriana 2

- The animal was not kept as a pet.

- It served a useful purpose.

- It was best not to walk around a Victorian kitchen in your bare feet.

Shammin' Famine

- The Russian journalist noticed something but it was not to do with the people he met.

- He noticed it on the journey from the airport to the city.

Come Home Quick

- This isn't related to safety, sports, voting, taxes, or health.

- The mayor wanted them back for the benefit of the city of Limerick.

- Their presence in the city on the Sunday evening counted for something.

I Spy

- The German spy was given away by something he did, not something he said.

- He wrote something down but used no German words.

- It was not words that gave him away.

Lying Dead

- The man died elsewhere.

- He appeared to have drowned.

- The dead man served a useful purpose.

- Deception was involved but no crime.

- This happened in 1943.

Passed With Extinction

- They are not alive.

- They are objects that were once common—even essential—but are now no longer needed.

Back Again

- The man did not forget anything or have any incomplete work-related business to take care of.

- He was not angry or upset.

- He was dismissed from his job for just cause and he was now out of work.

- His former place of work now served a new purpose for him.

Definitely Not

- The reporter had learned to speak basic Albanian, so the people he questioned understood what he was asking them.

- No one lied to the reporter or tried to mislead him.

- The reporter's language course had focused solely on spoken language.

Nervous Wreck

- The ship had been empty but was now full of water.

- The ship was positioned in such a way that hoists and cranes would not work. An inflatable float was suggested but not used; it would have been cut by sharp edges caused by the wreck.

Singles

- He did it to ensure that he was not cheated.

- The musician later became a world-famous singer and pianist.

Amadeus

- Mozart's entire body of work is popular with classical music lovers.
- He did not use obscure instruments for the fifth movement, or write it in a way that is difficult to play.
- The fifth movement was played in Mozart's time, but no one plays it today.

Let's Split

- This has nothing to do with religion, infidelity, or family matters.
- There was a major redevelopment plan for the village.
- The couples divorced for financial gain.

Elongation

- Ben was not wearing elevator shoes or a wig of some sort; for one week his body was actually physically longer than usual.
- He was not stretched in a rack or pulled in some way.
- His job is unusual, and he spent the week in an unusual place.

Ring-a-Ding

- The woman had recently come into money.
- This happened many years ago.
- The bell was in a place where you would not expect to see bells today.
- A bell used for this special purpose was very rarely rung.

Wet Coffee
- The water is not added for reasons of taste.
- The tradition began in order to improve safety and security.

Truffle Snuffle
- Dogs are not better at detecting the truffles than pigs are.
- The pigs bring a disadvantage with them.

Sell-by Date
- This food was buried with the pharaohs 4,000 years ago but when it was found it could still be eaten.
- It is not a meat, fruit, or vegetable.
- It takes thousands of workers to produce a small amount of this food.

Fly by Night
- Generally, someone should bring the flag down and take it in at the end of the day.
- There is one place where it is not possible to do this.

The Odd Day
- This does not have to do with anything that happens on Monday or its position in the week. It has to do with the word "Monday," which has a property that no other word for a day of the week has.
- This is a puzzle that a wordplay lover would be likely to solve.

Break the Fall

- The climber was a man but he was unusual.
- He broke his leg, but he was not in great pain.
- This is a true story of achievement in adversity.

Faint-hearted

- The man was looking forward to going home, but he did not faint in excitement.
- The nurse had been trained at a hospital in Sydney.
- He misunderstood what she said.

Pack Man

- This has nothing to do with planes or parachutes (that's a different puzzle!)
- His death was accidental and violent.
- The pack killed him directly but he was not poisoned, drowned, or crushed.

A Strange Count

- This does not involve leap years, international date lines, other planets, or any sort of device to alter time recording. He lived a normal 55 years.
- He died in the year 1984.
- He was born in a hospital.

Ready, Teddy

- This happened at a fairground.
- They wanted people to see that they had the teddy bears.
- It was a deception.

Strike a Light

- Babier found a way to communicate that did not involve light.
- His invention came to benefit certain people around the world.
- He invented a form of code.

Pay Dirt

- Their cell was inspected at the same time each day.
- They had to hide the dirt, but there was too much of it to smuggle it into the exercise yard, flush it down the toilet, or eat it.
- They used the limited resources available in their immediate environment.

Two Women

- The American woman was on a diet and it was successful.
- The same sentence could be applied to each woman yet the meanings would be quite different.
- The English woman became poorer.

Toy Wreck

- The nature of the cargo is relevant.
- The scientists learned things of value to them about the ocean.
- The toys were bath toys.

Just Four Words

- The words formed a simple grammatical sentence that would always change the King's mood.

- It is a prediction about change that is applicable to each of us no matter what condition we are in.

Murderous Intent

- She did not do this for any kind of financial gain.

- She had a seemingly rational reason for the cold-blooded murder of her sister.

- She was interested in the man she met at the funeral but she did not see her sister as a rival.

Ford Car

- They were unfamiliar with the area they were driving in.

- Their car had every modern accessory.

- They followed instructions to the letter.

Fair Enough

- The king asked for an appropriate musical cue.

- His instructions were misunderstood.

Hide and Seek

- The spy found a clever way to ensure that the codebook was not found during the police search.

- The police searched his house very thoroughly.

- It is a method that any of us could use if we knew that our premises were due to be searched on a certain day.

Monkey Business
- The monkeys perform a service for people.
- It seems unpleasant but it actually improves comfort and hygiene.
- Monkeys eat all sorts of things.

Unconventional
- Their religious order allowed spoken communication.
- They were allowed to greet each other, for instance.
- Certain words, however, were forbidden.

That Sinking Feeling
- He was a good swimmer but he drowned.
- He was rich.

Present Perfect
- The gifts were small, practical items. Customers were pleased with both gifts.
- They wanted the gifts to inspire people to order more products. The second gift was better suited to this purpose.

Hose Down
- The fire department thought that they were helping the plants.
- The plants were outside in a forest.
- The fire department did what the fire department usually does.

Something You Don't See Every Day

- The statue is in honor of inventing something that we have all encountered—but you could call it a big nothing.

- He introduced an innovation to a popular food.

More Murderous Intent

- The man shot himself in a park. He waited until there was no one around.

- No one assisted him in any way.

- He knew that if the gun were found next to his body it would look like suicide.

Red, White, and Blue

- The French team and their supporters would have preferred it if they had played in blue.

- Only one team was allowed to play in their traditional colors. The two teams tossed a coin before the match and the French lost.

- This has nothing to do with safety, security, fans, police, referees, or one team having an unfair advantage.

- It was done at the request of the TV companies.

Upgrade Upset

- John and Jane spent the flight in the first class section of the flight and were treated well by staff and passengers.

- They told a lie in order to get upgraded but the lie was not discovered.

Untouchable
- The signs were clear and people understood them.
- The people who touched the exhibits were not deliberately disobeying the instructions.
- Some people have to touch things.

Salt Fault
- The guest did not have any dishonest intent. He was trying to help his hostess.
- She had seen someone else acting suspiciously.

Burnt Out
- The woman had never met the man before.
- The woman was not upset because of the fire. She was upset because the man had observed the fire.
- It was a small fire.
- She deduced what the man had been doing. He was not a criminal.

The Angry Vacationer
- The man spoke to his neighbor before entering his home.
- The neighbor did not do anything or tell him anything that angered or upset him.
- He realized that he had lost something.

No Business Like Sideshow Business
- Barnum reputedly said, "There's a sucker born every minute."
- The customers saw acts that conformed to the descriptions but were not what they were expecting.

The Odd Shot

- The player wants to win the competition, but he deliberately takes a more difficult route to the hole knowing that it will almost certainly cost him a shot.
- The player is not trying to gain an unfair advantage—quite the opposite.
- This is his first shot of the day.

Cheers

- The bars did not know that he had cancer, and in any case his condition was not contagious in any way.
- The bars had a particular policy to encourage safety.
- His appearance changed as a result of his treatment.
- He was a young man given to wearing leather jackets and ripped jeans, although he would not normally have been banned for wearing such clothing.

Two Coats

- Kevin was following instructions—or so he thought.
- He was holding a brush.

Go With the Flow

- North and south did not change—the direction of the river changed.
- Water flows downhill.

No Charge

- The woman was acting with criminal intent.
- She had made the $200 bill.
- She could not be charged with counterfeiting.

Rival Arrival

- Antonia did not want to be seen in the same dress that someone else was wearing.

- Gwendoline arrived in the dress.

- No other guest wore the dress but Gwendoline was still very upset.

Skid Lids

- The helmets are effective in protecting people's heads in case of accidents. But it appears that they increase the likelihood of accidents.

- The problem does not lie with the cyclists, but with other road users.

Mouseophobia

- The mouse was not alive.

- It was the commonest type of mouse—found in many homes.

The Dunce

- Sammy was given a nickname that related to his poor mathematical ability.

- The nickname later became part of his stage name.

An Unwanted Purchase

- The woman was not happy to be doing this.

- After she bought the item she threw it away.

- She had not entered the shop with this purpose in mind.

Watch Out

- The restaurant was a special kind of restaurant. It emphasized taste and experience.

- The issue with the watch did not relate to time.

- Not every guest had to remove his or her watch.

The Unfriendly Man

- The man was not a criminal and his primary intention was not to harm the woman.

- He did not rob her but he took something she had.

- He struck her for his own benefit.

- He was an actor in the middle of a play.

Parking Lark

- He deliberately parked his truck at night some distance from his home and then he returned the next morning to drive it away.

- The lie was about Hugo.

- He acted in revenge.

Stuck Fast

- The explorer had enough food and water to last a week or so.

- He was lodged firmly in the hole, and was stuck in it waist-deep.

- He had no means of widening the hole.

What's the Hitch?

- The movie features James Stewart as the hero. He has a broken leg and watches other apartments from his window.

- Alfred Hitchcock was pleased with all the actors' performances.

- You can see the mistake he made if you watch the film carefully.

Unorganized

- The conference was well-run and perfectly well-organized.

- The newspaper made an understandable mistake.

The Inventive Survivor

- He found a source of air but he did not break any walls or windows.

- He did not have air tanks or unusual equipment of any kind.

- He survived by going into the bathroom, even though smoke was pouring into the bathroom.

Fishing Rods

- She was angry about something.

- She wasn't planning to tell anyone that she had done this.

- They weren't going to be her curtain rods much longer.

Staying Grounded

- He bought the ticket at a discount.
- Airports have certain things found nowhere else.
- He didn't lose any money by not taking the flight.
- This happened in December.

A Fishy Story

- The woman knows what he takes with him on his fishing trips and what he returns with.
- If he were having an affair and saying he was taking fishing trips as a cover story, then what would he be sure to do?

Curses

- The boy was having trouble with the lesson.
- There was another rule that the boy broke by swearing.
- If he had chosen a different word to swear with, the teacher would not have minded.

WALLY Test 2

Time for one more WALLY test. Remember, these are meant to be answered as quickly as possible. Give yourself two minutes to answer all ten, don't change any answers once you've written them down, then check the answer section to see how you did.

1. What happens to gold when it is exposed to the air?

2. Which pine has the sharpest needles?

3. Which is heavier, a full moon or a half moon?

4. How many cows does it take to change a light bulb?

5. What can circle the world while never leaving its little corner?

6. Two bodies have I, though both joined as one;
   But the stiller I stand, the faster I run. What am I?

7. What did the 0 say to the 8?

8. If the President of the United States, the Queen of England, and the Pope arrived at the White House, who would go through the door first?

9. Who won last year's Bangkok marathon?

10. Somebody who lives in New York is called American; somebody who lives in London is called British. What do you call somebody who lives at the North Pole?

Find the answers on p. 92.

PUZZLE ANSWERS

Well Done

The teacher was teaching the International Phonetic Alphabet. He asked the girl how you would say the letters B and J in this alphabet. She got the answer wrong, so he corrected her.

Twin Peeks

Josh is deaf.

Bee Trail

The woman was a tightrope walker. She was balancing on a rope high over a ravine when a queen bee landed on her nose. A swarm of bees followed the queen bee onto the poor woman's face. She lost her balance and fell to her death.

Can the Can

A man was driving a vintage car. He filled it up with unleaded gasoline, but this would have caused undue wear to this engine, so he had to buy a canister of a chemical containing lead (highly poisonous!) and add it to his tank.

The Bathtub Test

You should pull out the plug!

Defective Dismissal

The man is working on a building site. He complains that his wheelbarrow is going "squeak ... squeak ... squeak ... squeak." The foreman fires him because he says the wheelbarrow should be going "squeak squeak squeak squeak" if he were pushing it fast enough!

Dampened Spirits

The man was trapped in an avalanche. When pressed on all sides by snow you can easily lose your sense of direction. Some people burrow downwards to escape and perish. Wetting his pants showed him the direction in which liquid flows, which is always downwards, so he knew which way was up. (This is actually an official piece of advice in some skiing manuals.)

Buttons

Buttons were placed there to stop men from wiping their noses with their sleeves!

Stage Fright

The producers looked in the phone book and found people with the same name as well-known drama critics. They paid them to say flattering things about the play and quoted it in the ads. The public was fooled—for a while!

The Warm Prisoner

The man turns on the cold-water faucet in his cell. The water is exceedingly cold.

Tight Fit

The woman was an actress and she had to audition for a part in which she played a crippled woman in pain and distress. Wearing the painful shoes helped with her appearance and gait.

On the Loose

When on duty the pilots wear heavy helmets loaded with electronic equipment. Over a period they develop strong neck muscles and larger, more muscular necks. Since shirt sizes are determined by the collar size, the pilots need bigger shirts.

Fingered

The burglar is a beginner and not very bright. He used those gloves with the tops of the fingers cut off!

Lots of Dough

The baker's employees invented the Frisbee using upside-down pie tins, which they threw to each other as a pastime during their lunch breaks.

A Sight for Sore Eyes

During World War II, the RAF did not want the Germans to know they had radar. They circulated a rumor that their pilots were spotting German planes at night because of their fantastic eyesight brought about by eating lots of carrots!

Getting Away With Murder

The room is an elevator.

Sparkle

When Lyndon Johnson was an ambitious young man starting out on his career, he lodged in Washington, D.C. He wanted to meet as many people as possible. Each time he went to the washrooms in the morning to brush his teeth he was able to meet and talk to analysts and politicians who were also brushing their teeth. This was one of the techniques he used to build a big network of contacts.

Awfully Unlawful

In earlier times the main industry on Jersey was fishing. The fishermen, because they made nets, were good at knitting. In bad weather they would stay home and knit. Some of them were reluctant to return to sea. The Jersey government passed a law making it illegal for men to knit in order to promote the fishing industry. The law has never been repealed.

Bow Untied

Pierce Brosnan also played the role of James Bond in the Bond movies at that time. His contract with the movie company that made the Bond movies forbade him from appearing in any other films wearing a black tie or a bow tie done up. This was done to protect the Bond brand.

Ageism

Young people have better hearing than old people. In particular, they can hear higher frequencies. The authorities installed speakers that emitted an unpleasant high-pitched noise that the young people disliked but the old people could not hear.

Bad News

Jane heard the news that the actress had been burgled and had lost $2,000,000 worth of jewelry. She knew it was wrong because she was the burglar and had discovered most of the pieces were worthless.

Nipped in Nippy Weather

During heavy snow, neighbors noticed that no snow seemed to collect on his roof. They phoned the police. He'd had special heating installed in his attic to grow marijuana plants.

Victoriana 1

The bathing suit.

Victoriana 2

Hedgehogs were often kept in Victorian kitchens because they ate slugs, cockroaches, and other undesirable creepy-crawlies.

Shammin' Famine

The Russian journalist (who had experienced famine in Russia) noticed on the way into town from the airport that there weren't any leaves on the trees. The well-fed Westerners did not realize what that meant.

Come Home Quick

The match day was census day in Ireland. So many people left Limerick for the match in Dublin that if they did not return on Sunday night the registered population of Limerick would fall below the threshold for a city and it would lose its city status. (In the U.K. census, people register where they spend Sunday night.)

I Spy

In writing down a number, he wrote his 7 with a line across the middle, in the European style.

Lying Dead

This happened during World War II. The man, whose true identity is not known, died of pneumonia. The British Intelligence services organized an elaborate deceit to fool the Germans into thinking that the Allies planned to invade Sardinia and not Sicily. They gave the man a false identity as a major and a briefcase full of sensitive documents. They then arranged for the body to be washed up on the beach in Spain, apparently the result of an airplane crash. The Germans got access to the documents and were deceived into moving their forces to defend the wrong island. This event was the basis for the movie *The Man Who Never Was*.

Passed With Extinction

Telegrams sent in the U.S. The service was suspended in 2006, killed off by e-mail.

Back Again

The man who lost his job had been working in the unemployment office. The next morning he showed up at the office looking for a new job.

Definitely Not

In Albania nodding your head means "no" and shaking your head means "yes. "

Nervous Wreck

Tens of thousands of Ping-Pong balls were forced into the hold to displace the water. The ship then rose to the surface.

Singles

In the 1950s Ray Charles was just starting out on his musical career. He was a pianist in a band. When they were paid, since he was blind, he insisted on single dollar bills so that he could count exactly what he had received. Later, of course, he became a big star and a millionaire.

Amadeus

Mozart wrote five movements for the suite *Eine Kleine Nachtmusik* but the score for one of them has been lost. It was played in Mozart's time, but nobody today knows what it sounds like.

Let's Split

A major building scheme was taking place that involved demolition of houses. Married couples were compensated with a two-bedroom apartment; single or divorced people were compensated with a single-bedroom apartment. Divorced couples could get two apartments, become "reconciled," then live in one apartment and rent out the other. The authorities soon clamped down on the scheme.

Elongation

Ben was an astronaut. Under zero gravity conditions the human spine expands. Astronauts' space suits are designed to accommodate this lengthening.

Ring-a-Ding

In medieval times people were worried about the risk of being buried alive. (It happened!) So people were buried with a cord attached to their wrists. It was connected to a bell in the cemetery. This woman had inherited the family fortune when her elder brother died. When she heard the bell ring she knew that he was still alive.

Wet Coffee

Historically there were many vendettas and enmities in Cyprus between rival families and between Greeks and Turks. A popular method of assassination was poisoning. The poison could not be tasted in strong coffee. But if you added a little water to a poisoned coffee it would fizz. Adding water to coffee was a security device that has become a tradition.

Truffle Snuffle

Pigs have learned to eat the truffles!

Sell-by Date

Honey, which never goes bad—it is too sweet even for bacteria!

Fly by Night

On the moon.

The Odd Day

Monday is the only day of the week with a single-word anagram: DYNAMO.

Break the Fall

The climber was a double amputee who had two artificial legs. One of them broke so he replaced the broken rod with a spare he was carrying.

Faint-hearted

The nurse was Australian and had a heavy accent. The patient heard what she said as "going home to die" instead of what she meant, "going home today."

Pack Man

It was a pack of wolves.

A Strange Count

He was born in room 1947 of the hospital.

Ready, Teddy

The man and woman were walking around a fairground. One of the midway games involved trying to knock over a stack of tin cans to win a big teddy bear. But the game was fixed and it was almost impossible to knock over the cans. When people saw the man and woman carrying teddy bears they assumed that the two of them had won them at the game and were then more inclined to play themselves.

Strike a Light

Babier invented a way of sending messages as a combination of twelve dots raised from the paper, which could be read silently with the fingertips in the dark. Later Louis Braille took up the idea as a reading device for the blind and reduced the number of dots to six.

Pay Dirt

They hid the dirt in the tunnel. They stole some nylon sacks from the bakery and every day they dug dirt from the tunnel and put it into sacks in their cell. Before the daily cell inspection they stored the sacks in the tunnel. On the last day they pulled out all the sacks, which were found in their cell by the guards.

Two Women

They both lost ten pounds. The American woman became slimmer, the English woman became poorer.

Toy Wreck

The cargo consisted of hundreds of thousands of plastic ducks. They floated to the surface and then currents carried them across the Atlantic. The number of ducks that arrived at various points on the coast gave scientists valuable information about the strength and direction of Atlantic currents.

Just Four Words

The jester wrote "THIS ALSO WILL PASS."

Murderous Intent

She killed her sister in the hope of seeing the man again at the ensuing funeral.

Ford Car

The couple had used satellite navigation to plan their trip. It rightly told them that the shortest route involved crossing a certain river. What it neglected to tell them was that there was no bridge and the crossing was by ferry!

Fair Enough

The sound library was instructed that a "fanfare" was needed for the broadcast. The word "fanfare" was misinterpreted as "fun fair." (True incident!)

Hide and Seek

Very early in the morning he mailed the codebook to his own address. It was delivered safely the day after the police search failed to find it.

Monkey Business

Natives carry them on the tops of their heads; the monkeys keep head lice under control.

Unconventional

The nuns were told not to say "hello" because it contains the word "hell"! They were encouraged to say "heaven-o" instead.

That Sinking Feeling

One rich passenger trusted no one to look after his money, so he carried all his wealth with him at all times as gold bullion strapped around his waist. The weight prevented him from swimming clear of the ship to one of the lifeboats.

Present Perfect

They first provided a clock (and a blank order form) with each order. Later they tried including a pen with the order form instead. They found that customers were more inclined to reorder when they had a pen to write with.

Hose Down

The rare plants were giant sequoia trees (redwoods)—the largest living things on the planet. For many years the fire service put out forest fires thinking that by doing so they were protecting the trees. But sequoias have thick, fire-resistant bark, and sequoia seedlings have the best chance of survival after a fire when other plants are burned back and competition is reduced. Now small fires are allowed and managed in sequoia forests to allow growth.

Something You Don't See Every Day

Hanson Gregory reputedly invented the hole in the doughnut!

More Murderous Intent

He attached several helium balloons to the revolver and then knelt down and shot himself from above so that it looked like an execution. The gun floated away on the helium balloons. With no weapon at the scene, it looked like murder, not suicide.

Red, White, and Blue

The World Cup is very popular throughout the world and in many countries it is still commonly watched on black-and-white TVs. The colors red and blue look the same on black-and-white TVs.

Upgrade Upset

John and Jane were brother and sister who had booked economy tickets. They told the check-in clerk that they were a honeymooning couple and the clerk upgraded them to first class. During the flight it was announced that a honeymooning couple were in the first class cabin. People around them applauded and insisted that John give his "bride" a passionate kiss. They had to go through with the charade for the rest of the flight.

Untouchable

Part of the exhibit was a sign in Braille asking people not to touch the exhibit. Of course, blind people had to touch the sign to read it and thus find out they were not supposed to touch it!

Salt Fault

The story goes that Winston Churchill was approached by the hostess at an elegant party. She told him she had seen one of the other guests putting one of her antique salt shakers into his pocket and she did not know what to do. Churchill told her not to worry. He put a similar salt shaker in his own pocket, sidled up to the other man and, showing the salt shaker in his pocket, he said, "I think we've been spotted. We'd better put these back."

Burnt Out

The man was a policeman who was keeping the woman suspect under surveillance from across the road. When he saw smoke in her kitchen he phoned to warn her of the danger and she was angry to learn that she was being watched.

The Angry Vacationer

The man got out of his taxi and put his suitcase down at the end of the drive to his house. He walked down the road to speak to a neighbor. A garbage truck came along and his suitcase was thrown into the garbage and compacted.

No Business Like Sideshow Business

The "Man Eating Fish" was a man who was eating fish. The "Cherry-Colored Cat" was a black cat—the same color as black cherries.

The Odd Shot

The day before, the golfer was about to play a shot where a tree was blocking his view of the green, when an alert sounded to say there was danger of a thunderstorm and play was being suspended for the day. So he marked his ball. That night a huge bolt of lightning struck the tree and destroyed it. The next day, when he replaced his ball, he now had a clear view of the green but sportingly refused to take advantage of his good fortune and played the ball sideways onto the fairway as he intended to do originally.

Cheers

The man received chemotherapy treatment and all his hair fell out. Many bars have a policy of banning skinheads; he was mistaken for one.

Two Coats

Kevin was painting a door. The instructions on the can said, "Apply in two coats."

Go With the Flow

The Tonle Sap River in Cambodia flows north for part of the year and south for the other part. It connects a large lake to the Mekong River. After the monsoon the Mekong rises and the water flows back to the lake.

No Charge

There's no such thing as a $200 bill ($100 is the highest current U.S. denomination) so she was not counterfeiting anything. She was charged with attempted theft by deception.

Rival Arrival

Antonia wore a different dress and instructed her elderly maid to wear the original dress.

Skid Lids

The report found that motorists were more likely to hit cyclists wearing helmets. It seems that car and truck drivers assume that a cyclist wearing a helmet is more mature and predictable than other cyclists, therefore they do not need to give them a wide berth. This leads to more accidents.

Mouseophobia

Betty's cat had picked up a discarded computer mouse.

The Dunce

Sammy's full name was Samuel Mostel. According to one explanation of the origin of his nickname, "Zero," it was given to him by his classmates because of his low marks. In later life he became famous as the movie star Zero Mostel, partly due to his striking first name.

An Unwanted Purchase

The woman's young son broke a vase in a shop where all breakages had to be paid for. She reluctantly paid for the useless item.

Watch Out

The restaurant was deliberately in complete darkness. This was done as a "blind" experience, to encourage customers to focus on their sense of taste. The man's watch had a luminous dial so he was asked to remove it.

The Unfriendly Man

The man was a very vain old ham actor who would stop at nothing to sell a scene. At the climax of a play he came onstage with a false knife and a capsule of red liquid under his shirt. However, his assistant had forgotten to fill the capsule and nothing happened when he "stabbed" himself. Thinking quickly, he lurched into the wings, hit the face of the first person he saw (a female stagehand he didn't know), making her nose bleed profusely. He smeared the blood on his hands, chest, and knife and lurched back onstage.

Parking Lark

Hugo heard that a woman in the town had started an unpleasant rumor about him. He parked his distinctive pickup truck outside her house overnight so that other gossips might imagine that a man had stayed with her.

Stuck Fast

The explorer simply waits and doesn't eat his provisions, only drinking water to avoid dehydration; after a few days he starts to lose weight. He is then free to wriggle out.

What's the Hitch?

Rear Window features Jimmy Stewart's character laid up with a broken leg observing the goings-on in the apartments opposite his own. The "cast" in this puzzle refers not to the actors but to the cast on his leg, which in most scenes is on the left leg, but in one scene is on the right leg.

Unorganized

The conference was organized by the United Nations and was therefore UN-organized. A copy editor mistakenly printed the first part in lowercase and deleted the hyphen.

The Inventive Survivor

The shower head had a flexible hose; the man took it and pushed it through the water in the toilet basin. He breathed the air that was in the pipe beyond. The smoke did not pass through the water barrier.

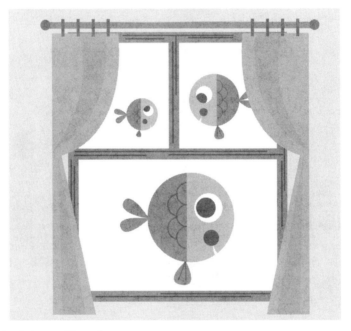

Fishing Rods

As part of her divorce settlement she had to vacate her house for her ex-husband and his new girlfriend. She pushed sardines inside the curtain rods, which caused a very unpleasant smell. Her ex could never figure out where the mysterious odor came from.

Staying Grounded

Patrick bought a low-cost ticket to a nearby foreign destination, checked in at the airport, and went through security to the departure lounge. He did all his Christmas shopping in the duty-free store and saved far more money than the ticket had cost. He waited until the flight had left and then apologized at the check-in counter for missing his flight. There was no other flight to the destination that day so he was sent home. Mission accomplished.

A Fishy Story

He never brings home any fish! If he weren't really fishing, he'd feel obliged to bring a fish home every once in a while to lend credence to his cover story.

Curses!

It was during a French lesson where all conversation was supposed to be spoken in French. The boy became frustrated and swore in English.

WALLY Test Answers

1. A carrot.
2. 4,100 (not 5,000, as most people say).
3. 0 or 3 or 4 depending on how you do it—horizontally, vertically, or mathematically.
4. Lassie.
5. Only one—ours, because only Earth can have earthquakes.
6. Horse racing.
7. Babies.
8. All the doors were locked.
9. In the dictionary.
10. Park in it, man.

WALLY Test 2 Answers

1. Someone tries to steal it.
2. A porcupine.
3. A half moon, because a full moon is lighter.
4. Don't be silly; cows can't change light bulbs.
5. A postage stamp.
6. An hourglass.
7. Nice belt!
8. No one would go through the door; they all go through the doorway.
9. It was a Thai.
10. Crazy!

INDEX

About the Authors

Paul Sloane lives in Camberley, Surrey, England. He has been an avid collector and composer of lateral thinking puzzles for many years. He runs the Lateral Puzzles Forum on the Internet, where readers are able to pose and solve puzzles interactively: **www.lateralpuzzles.com.**

Sloane has his own business helping organizations use lateral thinking to find creative solutions and improve innovation. The Web site is: **www.destination-innovation.com.**

He is a renowned speaker and course leader. He is married with three daughters, and in his spare time he plays golf, chess, tennis, and keyboards in an aging rock band, the Fat Cats.

Des MacHale was born in County Mayo, Ireland. He lives in Cork with his wife, Anne, and their five children. He's an associate professor of mathematics at University College Cork. He has a passionate interest in puzzles of all sorts and has written over 60 books on various subjects—lateral thinking puzzles, jokes, a biography of the mathematician George Boole, insights on John Ford's film *The Quiet Man,* and a nine-volume *Wit* series of humorous quotations. He has published puzzles in the Brainteaser section of *The Sunday Times* of London.

MacHale's other interests include bird-watching (ah, so relaxing), classical music and Irish traditional music, book collecting, photography, old movies, tennis, quizzes, words, humor, broadcasting, and health education. In fact, he's interested in everything except wine, jazz, and Demi Moore. (Our apologies to Ms. Moore.)

Paul Sloane and Des MacHale are the authors of eleven lateral thinking puzzle books for Sterling Publishing. More recent titles include *Cunning Lateral Thinking Puzzles, Classic Lateral Thinking Challenges, Colorful Lateral Thinking Puzzles, Great Lateral Thinking Puzzles, Improve Your Lateral Thinking, Intriguing Lateral Thinking Puzzles,* and *Brain-Busting Lateral Thinking Puzzles.*

WHAT IS MENSA?

Mensa®
The High IQ Society

Mensa is the international society for people with a high IQ. We have more than 100,000 members in over 40 countries worldwide.

The society's aims are:
- to identify and foster human intelligence for the benefit of humanity;
- to encourage research in the nature, characteristics, and uses of intelligence;
- to provide a stimulating intellectual and social environment for its members.

Anyone with an IQ score in the top two percent of the population is eligible to become a member of Mensa—are you the "one in 50" we've been looking for?

Mensa membership offers an excellent range of benefits:
- Networking and social activities nationally and around the world;
- Special Interest Groups (hundreds of chances to pursue your hobbies and interests—from art to zoology!);
- Monthly International Journal, national magazines, and regional newsletters;
- Local meetings—from game challenges to food and drink;
- National and international weekend gatherings and conferences;
- Intellectually stimulating lectures and seminars;
- Access to the worldwide SIGHT network for travelers and hosts.

For more information about Mensa International:
www.mensa.org
Telephone: +44 1400 272675
e-mail: enquiries@mensa.org
Mensa International Ltd.
Slate Barn
Church Lane
Caythorpe, Lincolnshire NG32 3EL
United Kingdom

For more information about American Mensa:
www.us.mensa.org
Telephone: 1-800-66-MENSA
American Mensa Ltd.
1229 Corporate Drive West
Arlington, TX 76006-6103 USA

For more information about British Mensa (UK and Ireland):
www.mensa.org.uk
Telephone: +44 (0) 1902 772771
e-mail: enquiries@mensa.org.uk
British Mensa Ltd.
St. John's House
St. John's Square
Wolverhampton WV2 4AH
United Kingdom

For more information about Australian Mensa:
www.mensa.org.au
Telephone: +61 1902 260 594
e-mail: info@mensa.org.au
Australian Mensa Inc.
PO Box 212
Darlington WA 6070 Australia